10 SECRETS TO BOOSTING SALES IN THE US MARKETPLACE

BARBARA DIAMOND

TABLE OF CONTENTS

INTRODUCTION

In today's competitive marketplace, businesses need to do everything they can to stand out from the crowd and boost their sales. But with so many businesses vying for consumers' attention, it can be difficult to know where to start. That's where this book comes in.

In "10 Secrets to Boosting Sales in the US Marketplace", we'll explore 10 proven strategies for boosting sales in the United States. From understanding your target audience to leveraging social media, we'll cover everything you need to know to succeed. And we'll do it all in an engaging, easy-to understand words.

CHAPTER ONE

KNOW YOUR TARGET AUDIENCE

Every business needs a target audience - a group of people who are most likely to buy their products or services. Without a target audience, businesses are shooting in the dark, hoping to hit their target but not knowing if they ever will.

In this chapter, we'll explore what a target audience is and how to find yours. We'll also look at some examples of businesses that have successfully targeted their audiences and increased their sales as a result.

What is a target audience?

A target audience is a group of people who are most likely to be interested in what you're selling. This group is defined by certain characteristics, such as age, gender, location, interests, and income level. By understanding who your target audience is, you can better tailor your marketing and advertising efforts to reach them.

This is important because it allows you to make the most of your marketing budget and maximize your return on investment. Plus, when you're speaking directly to your target audience, you're more likely to resonate with them and make a sale.

There are a few key strategies for finding your target audience.

Market research
This involves studying your industry and your competitors to see who they're targeting and how they're reaching them. You can also conduct surveys or focus groups to learn more about your potential customers and what they're looking for.

Google Analytics
Use analytics tools like Google Analytics to see who's visiting your website and what

they're doing there. This data can help you create buyer personas, which are detailed profiles of your ideal customers. This makes it easier to target your marketing efforts.

A buyer persona is a fictional representation of your ideal customer based on data and research. Creating a buyer persona involves answering questions like:
- Who is your ideal customer?
- What are their interests and hobbies?
- What is their lifestyle like?
- What are their needs and wants?
- How do they make decisions?
- What are their pain points?
Answering these questions can help you create a detailed profile of your target audience. With this information, you can better understand how to reach and connect with them.

Segment your target audience
This means breaking them down into smaller groups based on shared

characteristics. For example, you might segment your audience by age, gender, location, income level, or interests. This allows you to target your marketing efforts more effectively and make sure you're reaching the right people with the right message.

The takeaway is that understanding and targeting your audience is key to success. Without a clear target audience, your marketing efforts will be unfocused and ineffective. But with the right research and segmentation, you can reach the right people with the right message and drive sales.

CHAPTER TWO

UNDERSTAND YOUR COMPETITION

In business, it's important to understand your competition. Knowing who your competitors are and what they're doing can help you stay ahead of the curve and make better business decisions. This chapter will explore how to research your competition and what to look for when you do. We'll also cover some best practices for analyzing your competitors and using that information to your advantage.

The first step in understanding your competition is to identify who they are. This may seem obvious, but it's not always as simple as it sounds. You'll need to look beyond your direct competitors to also consider indirect competitors and potential future competitors.

Direct competitors are businesses that offer the same products or services as you. Indirect competitors are businesses that offer similar products or services, but may target a different market. Potential future competitors are businesses that could enter your market in the future.

Once you've identified your competitors, the next step is to research them. Start by looking at their websites and social media pages.

There are a few different ways to identify your competition.

1.Look at your customers and see what other products or services they're using. You can also do a Google search for keywords related to your business and see who comes up.

2. Look at industry reports and see who the major players are.

3. Talk to people in your industry and ask who they consider to be their competitors.

By using a combination of these methods, you should be able to get a good idea of who your competition is.

4. Look at your competitors' strengths and weaknesses. This will help you understand what they're doing well and where they might be falling short. You can then use this information to differentiate yourself from them and offer something unique.

You should also look at their pricing and marketing strategies. This will help you understand what you're up against in terms of pricing and how you need to position yourself in the market.

CHAPTER THREE

DEFINE YOUR UNIQUE SELLING PROPOSITION

The Unique Selling Proposition, or USP, is one of the most important things you can define for your business. It's what sets you apart from your competitors and makes you special. Without a strong USP, it will be hard to attract and retain customers. In this chapter, we'll discuss what a USP is and how to create one for your business.

Your USP is the single most important factor in determining your success. Without a clear and compelling USP, your business will struggle to stand out from the competition. It will be hard to attract customers and you'll be fighting an uphill battle to make sales. But with a strong USP, you'll be able to differentiate yourself from your competitors and give customers a reason to choose you over them.

What is a USP?

A USP is a statement that summarizes the unique value that your business offers to customers. It should be short and to the point, and it should be something that your competitors can't easily copy. Your USP should be based on what makes your business special and what makes you different from everyone else. It should be clear and easy to understand, so that customers can quickly grasp what you have to offer.

To define your USP, you first need to understand what makes your business special. What do you offer that no one else does? What makes you unique? Take some time to think about this and come up with a list of your strengths. Then, choose the one that you think is the most compelling and will resonate most with your target audience.

Once you've chosen your USP, you need to make sure it's reflected in everything you do, from your marketing to your customer service.

Let's break this down a bit more.

First, let's look at some examples of strong USPs. A classic example is Domino's Pizza's USP, "Pizza in 30 minutes or it's free." This USP is clear, memorable, and easy to understand. It sets Domino's apart from other pizza companies and gives customers a clear reason to choose Domino's over the competition.

Another great example is Geico's USP, "15 minutes could save you 15% or more on car insurance." This USP is simple, memorable, and easy to understand. It tells customers exactly how they can benefit from choosing Geico over another insurance company.

Now that we've looked at some examples, let's talk about how to apply this to your own business. Start by looking at your products or services and identifying what makes them unique. Then, think about who your target audience is and what they care about. What needs do they have that you can fulfill? Once you've identified these things, you can start crafting your USP. It should be short, simple, and to the point. It should also be something that your target audience can easily understand and remember.

How to make sure your USP is reflected in all of your marketing.
Make sure your USP is included in your tagline, slogan, and other branding materials. Then, make sure your website, social media profiles, and other online presence all reflect your USP. You should also make sure that your customer service is in line with your USP. If you're promising speedy delivery, for example, you need to

make sure your customer service is just as speedy.

Now you know how to create a strong USP and make sure it's reflected in everything you do. Remember, your USP should be clear, simple, and memorable. It should also be something that's relevant to your target audience and what they care about. If you can do all of that, you'll be well on your way to success!

Are you feeling confident about this? Just remember to stay true to your USP and make sure it's reflected in everything you do. Consistency is key when it comes to branding. Oh, and one more thing - don't be afraid to experiment and try new things. Sometimes the best USPs come from trial and error. So don't be afraid to take some risks and see what works best for you.

CHAPTER FOUR

DEVELOP A POWERFUL BRAND IDENTITY

Your brand identity is how your customers perceive your business. It's made up of all the elements that make up your brand, including your logo, colors, fonts, and tone of voice. A powerful brand identity is one that's consistent, recognizable, and reflective of your USP. In this chapter, we'll explore how to develop a powerful brand identity that sets you apart from the competition.

Here's what you need to know about developing a powerful brand identity

1.Define your brand values. What are the core values that your business stands for? These should be reflected in your brand identity.

2.Choose the right logo, colors, fonts, and other visual elements. These should all reflect your brand values and USP.

3. you need to create a tone of voice that's consistent with your brand. This includes the way you write and speak to your customers. If you can do all of these things, you'll have a powerful brand identity that will help you stand out.

You need to make sure you're consistent with your brand identity across all channels. This includes your website, social media, email marketing, and any other marketing materials you use. And, you need to keep your brand identity fresh and up-to-date. Trends change, and so should your brand identity.

Measuring the effectiveness of your brand identity? How do you know if it's actually working ?

To measure the effectiveness of your brand identity, you need to track several metrics. These include brand awareness, brand sentiment, and customer engagement. You can track brand awareness by measuring the number of people who recognize your brand and know what it stands for.

Brand sentiment is the overall feeling that people have about your brand, and you can measure it by looking at social media mentions and online reviews. Finally, customer engagement is how much your customers interact with your brand, and you can measure it by tracking website traffic, email open rates, and social media engagements.

Now that you know how to measure the effectiveness of your brand identity, you can make adjustments as needed. You may need to tweak your messaging, visuals, or tone of voice to get the best results. Just remember to keep your customers in mind as you make any changes.

What you need to know about protecting your brand identity

First, you need to monitor your online presence closely. This means regularly checking your social media accounts, Google results, and any other online platforms where your brand is represented. If you find any misrepresentation of your brand, you can take steps to have it removed. Second, you need to be proactive about building a positive reputation for your brand. This means being active on social media, responding to customer feedback, and putting out high-quality content.

The next step is to be consistent in your branding across all channels. This means using the same logo, colors, and tone of voice on your website, social media, and any other marketing materials. This will help customers recognize and trust your brand.

Finally, you need to be prepared to deal with any potential crises that could damage your brand. This means having a plan in place for how to respond to negative publicity. Do you feel like you have a good grasp on protecting your brand identity?

Evolving your brand identity

As your business grows and changes, your brand identity should evolve along with it. This means revisiting your brand values and messaging on a regular basis. If your business strategy or target audience changes, your brand identity should reflect that. It's important to stay flexible and adaptable as you build your brand. That way, you can continue to grow and succeed.

So, are you ready to keep your brand identity fresh and relevant?

The importance of being authentic

This means staying true to who you are as a business and not trying to be something you're not. Customers will appreciate your authenticity and are more likely to trust and support your brand.

The benefits of having a strong brand identity

-It can help you attract new customers. A clear and consistent brand identity will help people understand what you have to offer and how you're different from the competition.

-It can build loyalty among your existing customers. When people feel a connection to your brand, they're more likely to stick with you over time.

-It can increase the value of your business. A strong brand identity can boost your bottom line and make your business more attractive to potential buyers or investors.

-There are also benefits for your employees. When your employees feel proud of your brand, they're more likely to be engaged and productive. They'll also be more likely to recommend your business to their friends and family.

-A strong brand identity can help you attract top talent. People want to work for a company that has a clear mission and values.

-It can make you feel more fulfilled as a business owner. Knowing that your brand is making a positive impact can be very rewarding.

To sum it all up, a strong brand identity can help you;
-Attract new customers
- Build loyalty,
- Increase your business value,
- Engage employees,
- Make you feel more fulfilled.

Some potential challenges you might face when building your brand identity.

The first challenge is staying true to your brand. It can be tempting to change your brand identity to fit with the latest trends, but this can be a mistake. When you change your brand identity too often, people won't be able to recognize or trust you.

Another challenge is staying consistent across all channels. It's important to make sure your website, social media, and other marketing materials are all on the same page.

It can be difficult to stand out in a crowded marketplace.

How do you plan to overcome these challenges?

One way to stay true to your brand is to create a brand mission statement. This is a statement that outlines your core values and what you're trying to achieve as a business. It can be a great reference point when you're making decisions about your brand identity.

Another tip is to create a brand style guide. This is a document that outlines the specific colors, fonts, and other elements that make up your brand identity. Having a style guide can help you stay consistent across all channels.

Finally, it can be helpful to focus on what makes you unique. What is it about your business that sets you apart from the rest.

The benefits of having a strong brand identity for your customers.

1. it makes it easier for them to understand what you're all about. When they see your logo or hear your tagline, they'll immediately know what you're all about. This can build trust and loyalty.
2. It makes you more memorable. If your brand is consistent and easy to recognize, it will stick in people's minds.
3. It can make you more approachable. People are more likely to do business with a company that feels friendly and familiar.

The benefits for your employees.

1.It can increase their engagement. If your employees feel proud of your brand, they'll be more likely to be engaged and productive.

2.It can help you attract top talent. People want to work for companies that have a strong brand identity.

3. It can help with employee retention. When people feel connected to your brand, they're more likely to stay with your company for the long term. So, as you can see, there are many benefits of having a strong brand identity.

CHAPTER FIVE

CREATE ENGAGING CONTENT

Creating engaging content is an essential part of building a successful brand. Without engaging content, people won't be interested in what you have to say. In this chapter, we'll explore what it means to create engaging content. We'll also look at some examples of companies that do this well.

The first thing to know about creating engaging content is that it's all about your audience. You need to know who they are, what they care about, and what they want. Once you have a good understanding of your audience, you can start to create content that resonates with them.

This is the key to engagement. For example, a company that sells healthy snacks might create content about the benefits of eating healthy. They might share recipes, tips for eating on the go, or information about the ingredients in their products. By creating content that's relevant to their audience, they can engage.

Another key element of creating engaging content is **making it easy to consume.** People are busy, and they don't have time to read long, complicated articles. So, you need to make your content easy to understand and digest. One way to do this is to use clear and concise language.

You should also break up your content into short, digestible pieces. For example, you might use subheadings, bullet points, or numbered lists. This will make it easier for people to read and retain the information you're sharing.

Another important element of creating engaging content: **visual appeal.** In today's world, people are bombarded with visual content every day. So, you need to make sure your content stands out from the crowd.

One way to do this is to use high-quality images and graphics. You can also use infographics, videos, and other types of visual content. The goal is to make your content easy on the eyes and visually appealing. This will help people remember it and engage with it.

Another important aspect of creating engaging content is **emotion.** Emotion is what makes people take action. So, you need to use emotion to get people to connect with your brand. You can do this by telling stories, using humor, or appealing to people's emotions in other ways.

For example, a company that sells skincare products might tell stories about people who have had their lives transformed by their products. Or they might use humor to make people laugh and feel good about themselves. By using emotion, you can create a connection with your audience and get them to engage with your content.

The next thing to consider is **relevance**. Your content needs to be relevant to your audience and to the world around them. For example, a company that sells air purifiers might create content about the air quality in different parts of the world. Or they might talk about the health benefits of breathing clean air. This is relevant to their audience and to the world around them. Relevance is key to creating engaging content that people will want to share and discuss.

The final element of creating engaging content: **consistency.** In order to build a relationship with your audience, you need to be consistent with the type of content you create and the message you share. People need to know what to expect from you. So, you should create a consistent voice and tone in all of your content. This will make it easier for people to connect with your brand and to trust you. Consistency is key to building a strong and engaged following.

Some specific strategies to use to make your content more engaging.

STORYTELLING

Telling stories is one of the best ways to engage your audience. Stories are memorable and easy to understand. They can also create an emotional connection with your audience. So, when you're creating content, try to tell a story that relates to your audience and to the message you want to share.

For example, a company that sells security systems might tell stories about how their products have helped people feel safe in their homes. This will help people relate to the company and the products they sell. It will also help people remember the company and their message.

CREATE INTERACTIVE CONTENT

Interactive content is any content that people can participate in or interact with. This can include quizzes, surveys, polls, or games. Interactive content is great for engagement because it gets people involved and encourages them to share their thoughts and opinions. It's also a great way to learn more about your audience. For example, you could create a quiz about your products or services. This would help you understand what people are interested in and what they know about your brand.

CREATE CONTENT THAT'S SHAREABLE

People are more likely to engage with content that they can easily share with their friends and followers. So, when you're creating content, think about how you can make it easy to share. This might include adding social media share buttons or making it easy to email the content to a friend. You might also consider creating content that's funny, inspiring, or thought-provoking. This will encourage people to share it with their friends and followers.

The importance of quality; When it comes to engagement, quality is key. People are more likely to engage with content that's high-quality and well-written. So, when you're creating content, make sure it's well-researched, well-written, and free of errors. This will show that you care about your audience and that you're putting effort into your content. People will appreciate this and be more likely to engage with your brand.

CHAPTER SIX

OPTIMIZE YOUR WEBSITE FOR CONVERSIONS

In this chapter, we're going to talk about optimizing your website for conversions. This means making your website as effective as possible at getting people to take the actions you want them to take. For example, if you want people to sign up for your newsletter, you need to make it easy for them to do so on your website. We'll discuss how to optimize your website for conversions, and how to measure the success of your efforts.

The first step in optimizing your website for conversions is to identify your goals. What do you want people to do when they visit your website? Once you know your goals, you can create a plan to achieve them.

Next, you need to make sure your website is easy to navigate. People should be able to find what they're looking for quickly and easily. You should also make sure your website is mobile-friendly. More and more people are using their phones to access the internet, so it's important that your website is designed for mobile devices.

More specific strategies

1.Use calls-to-action (CTAs)

CTAs are prompts that encourage people to take a specific action, like signing up for your newsletter or making a purchase. You should use CTAs throughout your website, and they should be clear, concise, and action-oriented. For example, instead of saying "Sign up for our newsletter," you could say "Get our weekly newsletter." This is more direct and more likely to get a response.

2.Use persuasive copy

This means using words that will convince people to take the action you want them to take. For example, instead of saying "Join our mailing list," you could say "Get exclusive deals and coupons by joining our mailing list." This is more persuasive because it tells people what they'll get by taking the desired action.

3. A/B testing

This is a method of testing different versions of your website to see which one is more effective. You can test different elements of your website, like your CTAs, your copy, or your layout. By testing different versions, you can find the one that gets the most conversions.

4. Analytics

Analytics tools like Google Analytics can help you track how people are using your website. You can see which pages they're visiting, how long they're staying on your site, and what they're doing when they're there. This information can help you improve your website and make it more effective.

Some specific ways to use analytics. The first is to track your website traffic. This will tell you how many people are visiting your site, where they're coming from, and how they're finding you. This information can help you optimize your marketing efforts. For example, if you see that most of your website traffic is coming from social media, you can focus your marketing efforts on social media.

5. Conversion tracking

This is a way to track how many people are taking the desired action on your website. For example, if you want people to sign up for your newsletter, you can track how many people are doing that. This information can help you optimize your website to get more conversions.

6. Bounce rate

This is the percentage of people who visit your website and then leave without taking any action. A high bounce rate is not ideal, and it can be a sign that your website isn't meeting the needs of your visitors. You can improve your bounce rate by making your website more user-friendly, adding more relevant content, and reducing page load times.

7. Average time on page

This tells you how long people are spending on each page of your website. A low average time on page can indicate that people are not finding the information they're looking for. To improve this metric, you can make sure your website is easy to navigate, your content is relevant, and your page load times are fast.

8. Page views per visit

This tells you how many pages people are viewing on your website. A high page views per visit can be a sign that people are interested in your content and are exploring your website. You can improve this metric by making your website easy to navigate and by adding more relevant content.

9. Conversion rate

This is the percentage of visitors who take the desired action on your website. A low conversion rate can indicate that your website is not meeting the needs of your visitors. You can improve this metric by optimizing your website for conversions and making sure your content is relevant and compelling.

10. Click-through rate (CTR)

This tells you how many people are clicking on your ads or links. A low CTR can indicate that your ads or links are not relevant or interesting to your audience. You can improve this metric by creating more targeted ads and links.

Tips for improving your website's user experience.

-Make sure your website is easy to navigate and that your content is organized in a way that makes sense.

-Use clear and concise language on your website. Avoid jargon and technical terms that your audience may not understand.

-Use images and videos to make your website more visually appealing.

Tips for improving your website's content.

-Make sure your content is relevant and interesting to your audience.

-Use keywords and phrases that your audience is likely to search for. This will help improve your website's search engine optimization (SEO). Third, use calls to action throughout your website to encourage your audience to take the desired action.

Tips for improving your website's design.

-Make sure your website is mobile-friendly. This means that it looks good and works well on smartphones and tablets.

-Use a simple and clean design. This will make your website easier to navigate and more visually appealing.

-Use white space to break up your content and make it easier to read.

Best practices for improving your website's SEO

-Make sure your website is crawlable and indexable by search engines. This means that the search engines can easily read and understand your website's content.

-Use appropriate title tags and meta descriptions. These help the search engines understand what your website is about.

-Build links to your website from other websites. These are called backlinks, and they're an important ranking factor for SEO.

Some ways to improve your website's conversion rate

-Make sure your website's design is consistent with your brand. This will help your audience feel more comfortable and trust your website.

-Use social proof to show that your website is trustworthy. This can include customer testimonials, case studies, and trust badges.

-Use urgency to encourage your audience to take action. For example, you could use a countdown timer.

Another way to improve your website's conversion rate is to **personalize your website**. This means using dynamic content and personalization tools to tailor your website to each individual visitor. For example, you could show different content to visitors from different locations or demographics. You can also use personalization to show products or services that are relevant to each visitor.

Tips for improving your website's performance

-Test and optimize your website regularly. This means using analytics tools to track your website's performance and making changes based on the data.

-Focus on user experience. This means making sure your website is easy to use and provides a positive experience for your visitors.

-Be patient and consistent. It can take time to improve your website's performance, but it will be worth it in the end.

CHAPTER SEVEN

BUILD AN EMAIL LIST

Building an email list is an essential part of any digital marketing strategy. An email list is a database of email addresses of people who have opted in to receive emails from you. This is an extremely valuable asset for your business, as it allows you to stay in touch with your audience and promote your products or services.

In this chapter, we'll cover everything you need to know about building an email list, including how to collect email addresses, what to send in your emails, and how to grow your list over time.

Why you need an email list.

An email list gives you a direct line of communication with your audience. This is much more valuable than social media, where you're competing with other businesses for people's attention.

Email also has a much higher conversion rate than social media. In fact, email marketing has an average ROI of $44 for every $1 spent, making it one of the most effective marketing channels. Are you convinced that an email list is worth investing in?

How to start building your email list
1. Create a lead magnet. A lead magnet is a free resource that you offer in exchange for an email address. This could be a free ebook, checklist, or template. Whatever you choose, make sure it's valuable and relevant to your target audience. Once you have your lead magnet, you need to create a landing page. This is a page on your website where people can sign up to receive your lead magnet. Then, you need to promote your landing page. You can do this through social media, or your website.

2. Set up an email marketing service. This is a platform that allows you to send and manage your email campaigns. There are many different email marketing services to choose from, but some of the most popular options include MailChimp, AWeber, and ConvertKit. Once you've set up your email marketing service, you can start sending emails to your list. Your emails should be informative and valuable, and they should always include a call to action. The call to action could be anything from subscribing to your blog to buying your product.

Ways to grow your email list

One of the most effective ways to do this is to add a sign-up form to your website. You can place this form in the sidebar or at the bottom of your posts. You can also create a pop-up form that appears when someone visits your website.

Another way to grow your list is to add a call to action at the end of your blog posts. This could be a simple "subscribe now" button or a more creative call to action.

Finally, you can promote your email list through your social media accounts.

The importance of email segmentation.

This is the process of dividing your email list into smaller groups based on certain characteristics. For example, you could segment your list by location, interests, or purchase history. Segmentation allows you to send more targeted and relevant emails, which will result in higher open rates and click-through rates.

How to create effective emails

The first thing to keep in mind is your subject line. This is what will determine whether or not someone opens your email.

Your subject line should be clear and concise, and it should capture the reader's attention. You can also use personalization in your subject line, such as the recipient's name.

Next thing to consider is the design of your email. It should be visually appealing and easy to read. Use short paragraphs, bullet points, and images to make your email scannable. And finally, always include a call to action in your email.

One of the most important things to understand about email marketing is the concept of A/B testing. This is the process of testing different versions of your emails to see which one performs better. You can test different subject lines, call to actions, and even the time of day that you send your emails. By A/B testing, you can continuously improve your email campaigns and get better results.

Some of the dos and don'ts of email marketing

DO'S
First, do personalize your emails. People are more likely to engage with emails that feel like they're written specifically for them.

Second, do segment your list. This will allow you to send more relevant and targeted emails.

Third, do optimize your emails for mobile. More and more people are reading emails on their phones, so it's important to make sure your emails look good on all devices.
Fourth, do test different days and times to see when your audience is most engaged.

DON'TS

First, don't send emails without an unsubscribe link. This is not only illegal, but it's also bad for your reputation.

Second, don't send emails without permission. People are more likely to mark your emails as spam if they didn't sign up for them in the first place.

Third, don't overdo it with the images. Too many images can slow down your email and make it look unprofessional.

Fourth, don't use too many exclamation points or capital letters. This comes across as a spam.

How to measure the success of your email campaigns

There are several metrics you can track, but the most important ones are open rate, click-through rate, and unsubscribe rate. The open rate is the percentage of people who open your email. The click-through rate is the percentage of people who click on the links in your email. And the unsubscribe rate is the percentage of people who unsubscribe from your list. By tracking these metrics, you can determine what's working and what's not.

How to improve your open rate

-Make sure your subject line is relevant and attention-grabbing.

-Personalize your emails with the recipient's name.

-Send emails at the right time. The best time to send an email depends on your audience and your industry.

-Test different subject lines to see which ones get the most opens.

-Don't send too many emails. If you send too many, people are more likely to unsubscribe.

How to improve your click-through rate

-Make sure your call to action is clear and compelling.

-Make your email scannable by using short paragraphs, bullet points, and images.

-Don't bury your call to action at the bottom of your email. Place it near the top where it's more likely to be seen.

-Use strong and persuasive language to encourage people to click.

-Make sure your links are easy to click on, even on mobile devices.

The unsubscribe rate
This is the percentage of people who unsubscribe from your list. If your unsubscribe rate is high, it means people are losing interest in your emails.

There are a few things you can do to improve your unsubscribe rate.

-Make sure your emails are relevant and interesting.

-Givepeople the option to unsubscribe easily.

-Make sure your emails are not too frequent.

-Don't send spammy or misleading emails. By following these tips, you can keep your unsubscribe rate low.

CHAPTER EIGHT

LEVERAGE SOCIAL MEDIA

In this chapter, we'll discuss the basics of leveraging social media to promote your business. We'll cover the different platforms available, as well as best practices for creating and sharing content. We'll also look at how to track your success and measure the ROI of your social media efforts. By the end of this chapter, you'll have a solid foundation for using social media to promote your business.

An overview of the major social media platforms.

Facebook is the largest social network, with over 2 billion active users. It's a great platform for businesses to connect with customers and share news, updates, and offers. Twitter is a microblogging platform that allows you to share short, concise messages. It's great for breaking news, sharing links, and engaging with customers. Instagram is a photo-sharing platform that's perfect for visually appealing content. LinkedIn is a professional network that's great for B2B companies. And Snapchat is a popular platform among younger audiences.

Creating a social media strategy.
The first step is to set goals for your social media efforts. What do you want to achieve? Do you want to increase brand awareness, drive traffic to your website, or generate leads? Once you have your goals, you can create a content calendar. This is a schedule of what you'll share on each platform. Your content should be relevant to your target audience and aligned with your goals. Finally, make sure you're using analytics to track your progress. This will help you see what's working and what's not.

When creating content for social media, there are a few things to keep in mind

-Make sure your content is visually appealing. Use high-quality images and videos to grab attention.

-Keep your copy concise and to the point. People are more likely to engage with short, easy-to-read posts.

-Use hashtags to reach a wider audience. Hashtags are like keywords that make your content searchable.

-Always be authentic and engaging. People want to connect with real people, not just brands.

Specific tips for each social media platform

On Facebook, you should post a mix of images, videos, and links. Images tend to perform best on Facebook, so be sure to use them! You can also create a Facebook Page for your business. Pages are public profiles that allow you to post content and interact with your audience. On Twitter, you should post short, engaging tweets. Be sure to use hashtags and @mentions to reach a wider audience. You can also create Twitter Ads to promote your tweets. Instagram is all about visuals, so make sure your images are high-quality.

On Instagram, you should also post stories. Stories are a type of post that disappears after 24 hours. They're a great way to share behind-the-scenes content, and they tend to get more engagement than regular posts.

On LinkedIn, you should post content that is professional and relevant to your industry. LinkedIn also allows you to publish articles, which can be a great way to share your expertise.

On Snapchat, you should create fun, engaging content that's tailored to a younger audience.

Consistency is key on social media. Your followers will be more likely to engage with your content if they know what to expect from you. So, try to post regularly and maintain a consistent tone and voice. If you can do that, you'll be well on your way to social media success!

CHAPTER NINE

USE PAID ADVERTISING

While organic social media can be a great way to reach your audience, paid advertising can help you take things to the next level. With paid advertising, you can target specific audiences and get your content in front of more people.

There are many different platforms you can use for paid advertising, such as Facebook Ads, Google Ads, and Instagram Ads.

In this chapter, we'll take a look at the different platforms and how you can use them to reach your goals.

Facebook Ads

Facebook Ads are one of the most popular and effective ways to reach a target audience. Facebook has an incredible amount of data on its users, which allows for highly targeted advertising. You can target your ads based on demographics, interests, and behaviors. You can also choose to reach people who are already interested in your brand or product, or you can create custom audiences based on your website visitors or email lists.

Google Ads

Google Ads are a bit different from Facebook Ads. Instead of targeting specific audiences, you target specific keywords. When someone searches for one of your keywords, your ad will appear in the search results. Google Ads can be a great way to reach people who are already searching for what you have to offer. The great thing about Google Ads is that you only pay when someone clicks on your ad, so you're only paying for qualified traffic.

Instagram Ads

Instagram Ads are similar to Facebook Ads, but they have some unique features. You can target your ads based on demographics, interests, and behaviors, just like Facebook Ads. But you can also target by location, gender, age, and device. And with Instagram, you can create ads that look like native Instagram posts. This makes them feel more authentic and less like an ad.

Snapchat Ads

Snapchat Ads are quite different from the other platforms we've talked about. They're full-screen, vertical video ads that play automatically. They can be quite disruptive, but they're also very effective. You can target your ads based on demographics, interests, and behaviors. And you can also use Snap Audience Match to target people who have interacted with your website or app.

Best practices for creating successful ads.

-Make sure your ads are visually appealing. This is especially important on platforms like Instagram and Snapchat.

-Create ads that tell a story. People are more likely to engage with ads that tell a story rather than just selling a product.

-Use strong calls to action. Tell people what you want them to do after seeing your ad.

-Track your results. Use the analytics tools available on each platform to see how your ads are performing.

Budgeting

When you're creating your ads, you'll need to set a budget. There are two main ways to set your budget: cost-per-click (CPC) and cost-per-impression (CPM). With CPC, you pay each time someone clicks on your ad.

With CPM, you pay each time your ad is shown to someone. Which budgeting method you choose will depend on your goals and budget.

Optimization

Once you've created your ads and set your budget, you'll need to optimize your ads to make sure they're performing well. The first thing you'll want to do is test different versions of your ads. This is called A/B testing. You can test different images, headlines, and calls to action to see what works best. Second, track your metrics. Use the analytics tools available on each platform to track how your ads are performing. Third, make sure you're reaching the right people. Use targeting options to make sure your ads are being shown to the right.

Measuring success

When it comes to digital marketing, ROI is key. You need to make sure that your ads are generating a return on your investment. The first metric you'll want to look at is cost per acquisition (CPA). This is how much it costs you to acquire a new customer or lead. Next, you'll want to look at your conversion rate. This is the percentage of people who take the action you want them to take after seeing your ad. And finally, you'll want to look at your return on ad spend (ROAS).

Optimizing your landing pages

Your landing pages are where people end up after clicking on your ads. It's important to make sure your landing pages are optimized for conversions. There are a few things you can do to optimize your landing pages. First, make sure your headlines are clear and compelling. Second, use strong calls to action. Third, use images and videos to support your message. Fourth, include testimonials and social proof. Fifth, keep your forms short and sweet. Sixth, reduce distractions on your landing pages. Seventh, use A/B testing to optimize your landing pages.

Some common mistakes people make with digital marketing

-They don't have a clear goal or strategy. Without a clear goal, it's hard to know if your digital marketing efforts are successful.

-They don't know their target audience. Without knowing who you're trying to reach, it's hard to create effective ads and landing pages.

-They don't track their results. Without tracking your results, you won't know what's working and what's not.

-They don't test and optimize their campaigns.

-Not integrating their digital marketing efforts. Your digital marketing efforts should be integrated across all channels, including your website, social media, and email. This will help you create a seamless experience for your customers and prospects. It will also help you measure your results more accurately.

-Many people make the mistake of being too salesy. Your digital marketing efforts should be about building relationships and providing value, not just selling your products or services. Do you see how these mistakes can impact your digital marketing efforts?

Some common mistakes people make with specific channels, starting with social media

They don't post consistently. Consistency is key when it comes to social media. If you post inconsistently, your followers will lose interest and your reach will suffer.

They don't engage with their followers. Social media is a two-way street, and it's important to engage with your followers by responding to their comments and questions.

They don't use the right tone and voice. It's important to use a consistent tone and voice across all of your social media accounts.

Paid search advertising

This is a type of digital marketing that can be very effective, but there are some common mistakes people make. First, they don't have a clear goal. As we discussed before, it's important to have a clear goal for all of your digital marketing efforts. Second, they don't target the right keywords. If you don't target the right keywords, you won't reach your target audience. Third, they don't optimize their ads. Fourth, they don't track their results.

Best practices for digital marketing
Focus on quality over quantity. It's better to have a small, engaged audience than a large, unengaged audience.

Tell stories that resonate with your audience. Stories are a powerful way to connect with people and build relationships.

Be transparent and authentic. People want to do business with companies they trust.

Make it easy for people to take the next step. Always include a clear call to action. Last but not least, don't forget to have fun!

CHAPTER TEN

ANALYZE AND REFINE YOUR STRATEGY

As you've learned, digital marketing is an ever-evolving field. It's important to constantly analyze and refine your strategy to ensure you're getting the best results. In this chapter, we'll cover some of the key metrics you should be tracking and how to use them to improve your results.

The key metrics you should be tracking. These include:

- Website traffic - This is the number of people who visit your website. You can track this metric using tools like Google Analytics.

- Conversion rate - This is the percentage of people who take a desired action on your website, such as making a purchase or signing up for a newsletter.

- Customer acquisition cost - This is how much it costs you to acquire a new customer.

- Return on investment (ROI) - This is the amount of revenue generated from your digital marketing efforts, divided by the cost of those efforts.

How to use the key metrics listed above to improve your results.

Benchmark your current metrics so you have a baseline to compare against. Once you have a baseline, you can start to identify areas of improvement. For example, if your conversion rate is low, you may want to test different call to actions or make changes to your website design. If your ROI is low, you may want to adjust your budget or target different keywords.

Another important part of analyzing and refining your digital marketing strategy is testing. This is where you try different strategies and tactics to see what works best.

There are many different things you can test, such as:
- Ad copy - This is the text in your ads. You can test different headlines, descriptions, and calls to action to see what resonates best with your audience.
- Landing pages - This is the page people are taken to when they click on your ad. You can test different layouts, images, and copy to see what converts the best.
- Channels - You can test different digital marketing channels, such as search engine optimization (SEO), pay-per-click (PPC) advertising, and social media. By testing different channels, you can determine where you're getting the best results.
There are many other things you can test, but these are some of the most common.

Just remember, you should only test one thing at a time so you can accurately measure the results.

Some best practices for testing.
First, make sure you have enough data to make an informed decision. Second, be patient and give your tests enough time to run. It can take weeks or even months to see meaningful results. Third, make sure you're testing in a controlled environment.

This means you shouldn't change anything else on your website or ad campaign while you're running a test. If you do, it will be hard to tell what's causing the change in results. And fourth, use A/B testing software to help you track and measure your results. There are many different tools available, such as Google Optimize and Optimizely.

Some best practices for improving your SEO.

First, make sure your website is optimized for search engines. This includes using keywords throughout your website, having a fast and mobile-friendly website, and building backlinks. Second, create high-quality content that's relevant to your target audience. Third, make sure your website is easy to navigate and user-friendly. Fourth, use structured data to help search engines understand your content. And finally, be patient - it can take time to see results from your SEO efforts.

Best practices for PPC advertising

First, make sure your ad copy is relevant and compelling. You want to grab the attention of your target audience and encourage them to click on your ad. Second, target the right keywords. This is key to ensuring your ads are shown to the right people. Third, use negative keywords to exclude irrelevant searches. Fourth, set a reasonable budget and monitor your ad spend. Fifth, use conversion tracking to measure the effectiveness of your ads.

Best practices for social media

First, make sure your social media profiles are complete and optimized. This includes having a complete bio, a clear profile picture, and a link to your website. Second, post consistently and engage with your followers. Third, use hashtags to increase your reach. Fourth, use social media advertising to target your ideal audience. Fifth, analyze your social media performance to see what's working and what's not.

CONCLUSION

You now have 10 secrets to boosting sales in the US marketplace! You know how to craft a compelling offer, use social proof, build credibility, identify and target your ideal customer, create valuable content, use segmentation and automation, optimize your website and emails, and measure and analyze your results. These strategies can help you take your business to the next level and increase your sales. Thank you for reading, and I wish you success in all your future marketing endeavors.